It's Your Health!

Drugs

Jonathan Rees

FRANKLIN WATTS
LONDON•SYDNEY

First published in 2004 by Franklin Watts
96 Leonard Street, London EC2A 4XD

Franklin Watts Australia
45-51 Huntley Street
Alexandria, NSW 2015

Series editor: Sarah Peutrill
Editor: Sarah Ridley
Designed by: Pewter Design Associates
Series design: Peter Scoulding
Illustration: Guy Smith, Roger Stewart, Michael Courtney
Picture researcher: Sophie Hartley
Series consultant: Wendy Anthony, Health Education Unit, Education
Service, Birmingham City Council
Picture credits:
AP Photo/Dusan Vranic: 38. © Paul Baldesare/Photofusion: 9t. Steve
Bell/Rex Features: 17t. Photo from www.JohnBirdsall.co.uk: 37t. Peter
Brooker/Rex Features: 24. Paul Brown/Rex Features: 28. BSIP,
Chassenet/Science Photo Library: 37b. Dr Jeremy Burgess/Science Photo
Library: 27t. A. Crump, TDR, WHO/Science Photo Library: 33t. Andrew
Dunsmore/Rex Features: 35t. © Colin Edwards/Photofusion: 21. Chris
Fairclough/Franklin Watts: 4, 13, 15b, 17b, 19, 29b, 32, 40, 45.
Franklin Watts: 23t. © Melanie Friend/Photofusion: 11. David Hoffman
Photo Library/Alamy: 25b. Image Source/Alamy: 8. Dr P.
Marazzi/Science Photo Library: 39. © Naki/PYMCA: 30. © Mikkel
Ostergaard/Panos: 41t. PA Photos: 22. Photos/EPA: 20, 29t, 35b. ©
John Phillips/Photofusion: 14. Lee Powers/Science Photo Library: 27b.
Antonia Reeve/Science Photo Library: 33b. Leon Schadeberg/Rex
Features: 26. Science Photo Library: 10. © Houston Scott/Corbis Sygma:
12. SIPA/Rex Features: 9b, 31. © Paula Solloway/Photofusion: 23b. ©
David Tothill/Photofusion: 41b. © David Turnley/Corbis: 25t. © Libby
Welch/Photofusion: 34, 36. © Lisa Woollett/Photofusion: 8, 15t.

A CIP catalogue record for this book is available from the British Library

ISBN 0 7496 5566 6

Printed in Malaysia

Contents

What are drugs?

A drug is a substance or chemical that changes the way your mind or body works. Drugs are always in the news, and when we hear them mentioned, we may immediately think of drugs such as cannabis and heroin. But there are thousands of different drugs around the world, which are used by millions of people for many different reasons.

Taking legal drugs, like alcohol, is a socially-acceptable form of relaxation for millions of people.

Drugs and you!

You have probably already taken several drugs during your lifetime. Medicines like paracetamol and antibiotics are drugs that help you get better if you are unwell. Tea, coffee and chocolate contain a stimulant drug called caffeine. You almost certainly know people who drink alcohol and smoke tobacco. These are also drugs.

Some drugs are illegal. These drugs, such as cocaine, cannabis and ecstasy, are taken to change how you feel or think. They are also known as 'drugs of abuse' or 'recreational drugs'.

Medicinal drugs bring relief to almost everyone at some point in their life.

It's your experience

'Two years ago my friend and me sniffed some stuff we found in my dad's shed. We felt really strange and only tried it a few times. Then at school this teacher told us all about 'glue-sniffing' – how it was like taking drugs and was really dangerous. I hadn't thought of it like that before and I don't think I'll do it again'.

Shazad, aged 13

Where do drugs come from?

Some drugs are manufactured in factories and some come from mineral and animal extracts. Many illegal drugs are produced from plants, some of which will only grow in certain parts of the world. Cocaine and heroin, for example, come from plants grown in a hot climate.

Sometimes household products are used as drugs. Some people inhale the vapours rising from glues, gases and aerosols to get a good feeling, or 'high'. This is called solvent abuse and it is extremely dangerous.

Heroin, opium and morphine are produced from poppies grown in countries like Afghanistan.

It's your opinion

Alcohol and tobacco are drugs because they change how we think and feel. Why do you think most people don't consider them as drugs and will happily go to the pub for a drink or buy cigarettes from a shop? Is it because they are legal, or because they have been used for hundreds of years? Are there other reasons?

Drugs of abuse

There are many different kinds of drugs of abuse. Around the world it is against the law to use almost all of these drugs, so they are also known as illegal drugs. The illegal drugs we are most likely to hear about are amphetamines (or speed), cannabis, cocaine, crack, ecstasy, heroin, LSD (acid) and magic mushrooms. There are also many other drugs of abuse that are not as widely used.

'Hard' and 'soft' drugs

Sometimes illegal drugs are described as 'hard' or 'soft', depending on their effect. Heroin, for example, is considered to be a hard drug because it can be dangerous and addictive. Cannabis is generally thought of as a soft drug because it is not as dangerous or as addictive. Worldwide, opinions vary on how serious a problem it is to smoke cannabis (see pages 26-27).

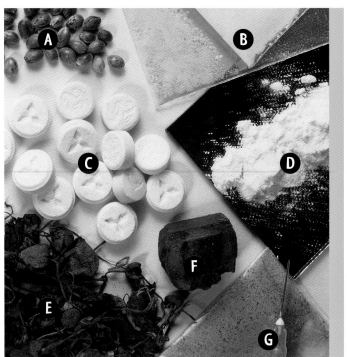

A Cannabis seeds
B Amphetamine
C Ecstasy pills
D Cocaine
E Magic mushrooms
F Cannabis resin
G Needle for injecting heroin

What do drugs look like?

Cannabis is usually a brown resin, which users smoke in cigarettes or pipes, though it can also be eaten. Cocaine is a white powder that is sniffed through the nose. Amphetamines can also be sniffed, as well as eaten as tablets. Ecstasy is usually in the form of tablets or pills, and LSD can be taken as tablets or small squares of paper. Heroin is a brown or white powder that can be smoked or injected into the bloodstream, using a syringe, and magic mushrooms are a type of fungus, eaten dried or fresh.

It's your experience

'I find the whole drug thing really scary. I know my big brother and his friends have taken drugs before, and I know loads of other people who don't think drugs are a big deal. I hope I don't start feeling the same way about it all.'

Sara, aged 11

Drug	Other names (slang)
amphetamine	speed, wizz, P, base
cannabis	marijuana, blow, ganga, grass, dope, weed, pot, resin, reefer
cocaine	coke, snow
crack (crystalline cocaine)	base, rock
ecstasy	E, doves, MDMA, disco biscuits
heroin	smack, gear, skag, junk, H
LSD (lysergic acid)	acid, tabs, trips
magic mushrooms	shrooms, mushies

It's your opinion

A survey in the UK in 2002, found that almost a half of all those aged between 16 and 24 had taken drugs at least once in their lives. One of the main dangers they face is that illegal drugs, unlike legal drugs, are not safety-checked so people cannot really know what they're buying. Why do you think they take drugs anyway?

Where do people get drugs from?

Because thes drugs are illegal, you cannot buy them in shops. People who sell them are known as 'dealers' or 'pushers' and they buy the drugs from other dealers and drug producers. Selling drugs makes some people, and even some countries, extremely rich as drugs are expensive to buy. For example, 80 per cent of all the cocaine used in the world is produced in Columbia, and it is one of the country's biggest money earners, netting at least $1 billion each year.

There may be a very long chain of people buying and selling, extending from where the drug originates to those who use it. When someone buys and sells drugs in this way they are breaking the law. If caught, punishments range from cautions and fines to lengthy prison sentences.

Dealers who sell drugs may be people you know, even your friends. ▶

11

What do drugs do to the mind?

People take drugs to change how they think or feel. These changes happen because chemicals in the drug act on the central nervous system in our body and affect how the brain works. It is important to realise that, as individuals, our bodies react differently to drugs.

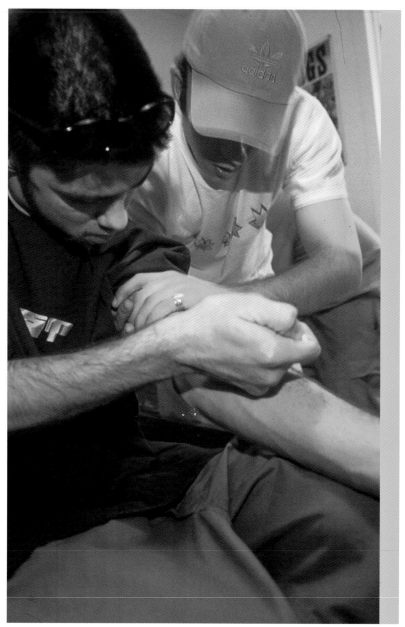

Addicts often inject drugs to get the maximum effect.

How are they taken?

For a drug to have any effect on you, it has to enter your bloodstream, which carries the drug to the brain. This can happen in different ways, depending on what form the drug is in. Smoking or sniffing a drug usually has a very quick effect, which tends to wear off fairly fast. Drugs such as cocaine and speed are often sniffed, or snorted, through the nose.

Other drugs, such as LSD, ecstasy and magic mushrooms, are swallowed. It usually takes longer for these drugs to take effect but the effect tends to last longer.

Injecting drugs, such as heroin, directly into the bloodstream is the most dangerous way to use drugs. It has very fast and powerful results that can last a long time.

Some drugs can be taken in a variety of ways. Cannabis, for example, can be smoked or eaten, resulting in different effects.

How do drugs make you feel?

Different drugs produce very different feelings because of the various ways they act on your body. Stimulant drugs, like cocaine, ecstasy and speed, increase brain activity, making you feel more alert and awake.

Depressant drugs, like heroin, have the opposite effect, making people feel calmer and more relaxed. Tranquillisers (medicines that calm you down) such as barbiturates and temazepam are also depressant drugs. These are not illegal when prescribed by a doctor, but are sometimes abused by drug users.

Hallucinogens are drugs that distort the way you see and hear things and even how you perceive time. They include cannabis, LSD and magic mushrooms. Solvent abuse can also have an hallucinogenic effect.

Exactly how a drug affects you depends on many things like the strength of the drug, your size and even your mood. If you are not used to taking drugs, or you mix different drugs, the effects may be very unexpected.

This 'stoned' drug user is unaware of the world around him. ▶

It's your decision

The decision whether to try drugs is ultimately yours. You have to decide whether it's worth risking your health. If you do decide to try drugs, you should at least take some precautions:

* Be as informed as you can so you are aware of what to expect. You could contact the agencies on page 43 for advice. For example, if you are taking ecstasy - do you know how much water to drink and when to 'chill out'?
* Don't take drugs on your own, make sure you are with someone you trust who is not taking anything, so they can help you if you have a bad reaction.
* Choose a place where you feel comfortable and safe.
* Be as responsible as you can. Every time you take something be aware of how your body feels before and after.

It's your opinion

Why do you think that some people choose to take drugs of abuse and other do not? What do you think is the main influence on a person's decision to lead a drug-free lifestyle – their health, the fear of being caught, or some other reason?

Why do people take drugs?

You might think that drug use is a fairly modern trend, but people have been taking drugs of different sorts for thousands of years. As far back as 8,000BCE, native Central Americans used mescal beans as a strong stimulant. Cannabis has been taken for at least the last 5,000 years, originally in Central Asia and China. Even the use of opium, the ingredient for heroin, dates back thousands of years, when it was used for pain relief and relaxation.

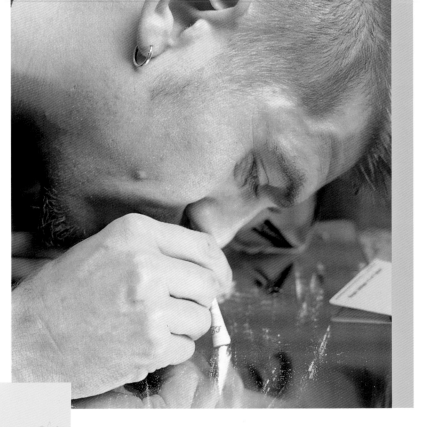

Cocaine is cheaper today than a few years ago but is still a very expensive habit.

Drug-taking today

Drug-taking has increased over the past 20 years. At the same time, the age at which people first use drugs has got lower. One reason for this increase is that drugs are cheaper and more easily available than in the past. It is difficult today not to come across drugs at some point in our lives.

It's your opinion

Some young people say they take drugs because they are bored.
Is this just an excuse? Can you think of ways that young people could escape from that boredom? Maybe there are other reasons for drug-taking that you can think of?

If you take a drug it will change the way you feel or think. Understandably, some young people are curious to see what effect it will have on them, and many will find they enjoy it – at least at first. Experiencing new things is, after all, an important part of growing up. The fact that many drugs are illegal adds to their appeal, and taking them can seem rebellious.

In some places like nightclubs, drugs are often widely available.

It's your experience

'I hadn't smoked cannabis before I went travelling and experimented with hash lassi (a cannabis yogurt drink). At first nothing happened then I just went out of control – shut myself in a toilet, nearly jumped off a roof and wandered off into the night. Luckily my boyfriend followed me and guided me to our room!'

Sarah, aged 21

Modern life

Maybe the way we live today drives people to taking drugs; after all, life at school, problems with your family and even dealing with your friendships can be very stressful.

Also if your friends, brothers or sisters take drugs it can very difficult to avoid them. Saying 'No' to people you like can be extremely hard when you probably just want to be one of the crowd.

Escape

Some people see drugs as a way of escaping problems in their lives – perhaps they are neglected or hurt by people around them. After a while, however, they may find that drug abuse itself becomes their greatest problem.

Your friends may influence your decision whether to try drugs.

Illegal drugs and physical health

There is no escaping the fact that taking illegal drugs puts our health in danger. Many people take drugs with no obvious damage to themselves but sometimes the consequences can take months or even years to appear. Just because one person's health appears unaffected by drug use does not mean the same will be true for you or anyone else.

It's your decision

Do you want to lose control?
If you take a drug you lose some control of how your mind and body works. This can be exciting to some people, while others fear this loss of control. After all it puts them at greater danger of being involved in an accident or becoming the victim of a violent crime, such as a mugging.

Some possible health effects of drug use

Cocaine and amphetamines can cause sleep disturbance.

Cocaine use can destroy the septum – cartilage in the nose.

Ecstasy can cause tiny blood vessels to overheat leaving red marks on the skin, especially the face.

Ecstasy can lead to liver failure, particularly if taken with other drugs such as alcohol.

Injecting heroin can cause veins to collapse, particularly in the arms.

If heroin users share needles they risk catching hepatitis, a disease that can damage the liver.

Ecstasy users may risk swelling in the brain due to drinking too much water in order to avoid dehydration (water loss). In the long-term it's possible that ecstasy may cause depression, anxiety and permanent brain damage.

Cannabis is more carcinogenic than tobacco and can irritate the throat and lungs.

Cocaine and amphetamine use can lead to heart damage.

Ecstasy causes the heart to speed up, which could lead to overheating and dehydration, and possibly unconsciousness. Users should drink a pint of water an hour and chill out regularly (but see above).

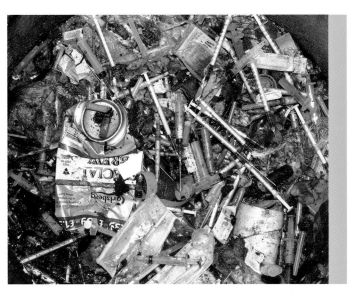

Dirty needles are a huge risk for drug takers. Health workers encourage addicts to swap their old syringes for clean ones at needle exchanges,

It's your opinion

Are the negative effects of illegal drugs over-stated? In the UK, as many as 150,000 people die from smoking and drinking alcohol each year, far more than those who die from illegal drug use.

Other risks

There are other risks related to drug-taking that are less obvious. Injecting repeatedly into veins can cause them to collapse. Sharing needles with other heroin users can pass on potentially deadly diseases, such as HIV, or hepatitis.

Sometimes drug-dealers mix or 'cut' drugs with other cheap and possibly dangerous chemicals so that they can make more money.

Can drugs kill?

Drug abuse can be a killer – more often for long-term drug users, but occasionally first-time users can die from an overdose or reaction. An overdose is when too much is taken too quickly or a drug is purer than normal so too much enters the body. With illegal drugs you can never be sure what is actually in them.

Certain drugs, like cocaine, raise the heart rate and blood pressure and so are very dangerous for people with an existing heart condition.

Because our bodies are all different, people react in different ways to drugs. It is known that mixing drugs with alcohol can lead to dangerous reactions in the body. In the UK around 3,000 people die each year as a result of using illegal drugs. Drugs are responsible for about 1,000 deaths in Australia and at least 10,000 deaths in the USA each year.

Hard drugs, such as heroin, cause most drug-related deaths although solvent abuse is the leading cause of drug-related deaths in children and young adults, a high proportion from first-time use.

Illegal drugs and mental health

It isn't just your physical health that could be at risk from drug use. In recent years, scientists and health workers have been looking into the effect that drugs can have on mental health and the way our minds work.

The brain

The human brain is an extremely complicated and finely balanced organ. It is continually reacting to different things happening around us to control our bodies and determine how we think and feel about things. One reason that people take illegal drugs is to change how their minds work, and experience new feelings. Sometimes, though, the brain reacts in unexpected ways.

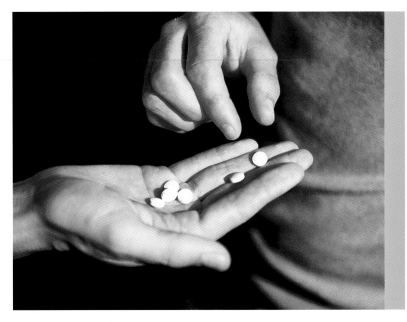

People who take ecstasy a lot risk developing mental health problems. Some users have problems when they are using ecstasy, but others may not feel the effects until years later.

It's your experience

'I'd heard about the 'midweek blues' from friends who had taken ecstasy but I reckoned it was a bit of a myth. But the first time I had a really heavy weekend with 'E' I saw what they meant. Come Tuesday I was so down I thought I'd never feel okay again. Luckily I felt better by the next weekend though.'

Cath, aged 14

Bad trip

You may have heard someone talking about having a 'bad trip' when they have taken a drug. This usually refers to the panicky feelings and nightmare visions after someone has taken a hallucinogenic drug like LSD. Sometimes users get 'flashbacks' where these feelings come flooding back; this may happen months or even years later.

Paranoia

Cannabis, and other drugs, can make users feel anxious and paranoid – worried that people are talking about them or making fun of them. This is more likely if you were not in a good mood when you took the drug. If you do have a bad reaction to a drug there is nothing you can do but wait for it to wear off.

Feeling high

Many drugs, including cocaine and ecstasy, can make you feel 'high' – on top of the world. You may feel in love with everyone, leading to actions that you regret later. Also, during a high, people often feel able to do absolutely anything – such as fly through the air or drive a car (even if they haven't passed their driving test).

It's your decision

Do you want an artificial high?
Many drugs, including alcohol, make you feel high for a while. But that feeling has been artificially created by the drug. Some people also take ecstasy, for example, so that they can keep awake for longer - therefore ignoring their body's signal that they need to rest.

Feeling low

After the effects of stimulant drugs like cocaine, speed or ecstasy have worn off, a user is likely to feel quite low, energy-less and depressed. Coping with normal life – the good bits and the bad – can seem unbearable. Some scientists now think that long-term use of ecstasy can result in permanent damage to the brain and cause mental illness in later life. Regular ecstasy users are 25 per cent more likely to suffer a mental health problem than the rest of the population. Long-term use of most drugs is now known to affect memory and concentration.

Along with the 'highs' many drug users have to put up with feeling low.

Drug addiction and dependence

When something is addictive it means that once you start taking it, it can be very difficult to stop. This is because your mind or body starts to need chemicals in the substance just to feel normal. Nicotine, the drug found in tobacco, is highly addictive; just ask any ex-smoker and they will tell you how difficult it was to give up. Alcohol and caffeine can also be addictive if taken regularly.

Even rich and famous people can have drug problems. Actor Robert Downey Junior has a string of drug convictions, and has struggled to break free from his addiction.

It's your opinion

Do you think that anyone can become addicted to drugs? Maybe you think only a certain type of person succumbs to addiction? Why do some people use addictive drugs even though they probably know the dangers?

Are illegal drugs addictive?

One of the more worrying things you may have heard about drugs is that they can be addictive. This is not true for all drugs but is certainly the case for some of them. One of the main problems with heroin, for example, is its addictiveness.

Heroin

People who use heroin usually start with fairly small amounts, but as time passes they have to use more and more to get the same effect. After a while they may well find that the 'good' feelings from using the drug have largely worn off. Now, if they don't take the drug, they start to get extremely unpleasant withdrawal symptoms (see pages 24-25) and taking it merely makes them feel normal again.

Heroin addiction is a major problem across the world. In 2003 there were some 40,000 registered heroin addicts in the UK, and more than 500,000 regular users of the drug in the USA. Around 240,000 Australians over the age of 14 have used heroin at some point in their lives.

▼ An addict prepares his next fix. For heavy drug users life revolves around getting hold of and taking drugs.

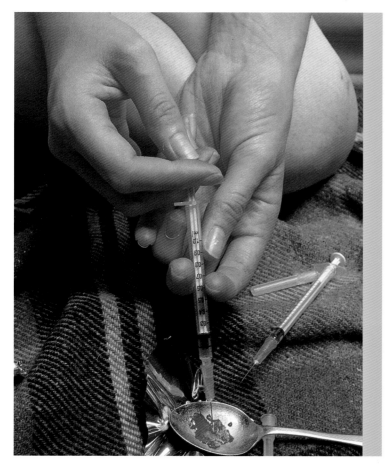

Dependence

Even drugs that are not physically addictive, such as ecstasy and cannabis, can still make you dependent on them. Regular users often feel that they need the drug to cope with or even enjoy certain situations. The same can be true for the legal drug alcohol, and for any other drug. This is known as psychological dependency.

A gateway to other drugs?

Many countries are debating how to view the less dangerous drugs, like cannabis. In the 1980s, one theory was that smoking cannabis would inevitably lead to the use of harder drugs. Recent statistics suggest this is not the case. Although it is true that almost all heroin users started their drug-taking by using cannabis, only a small proportion of cannabis users ever try heroin or other hard drugs. On the other hand, the dealer who sells cannabis may sell other drugs, and may persuade the cannabis user to try them.

Drugs education

At some time in your life you will learn about drugs and their possible dangers. This may be from your parents or teachers, from watching a programme on television, or reading this book. Drugs education comes in many forms, but does it help prevent or reduce drug-taking in young people?

Education in schools

When drugs education started in schools the message was generally very simple. Young people were told not to take illegal drugs under any circumstances because they were very dangerous. Despite this, drug use has increased for all age groups, so those in charge of drugs education realised that this approach was not working.

Some teachers and drugs workers believe that drug education should start at an early age.

It's your experience

'We had this woman talking to us about drugs at school recently. She was really cool and didn't make out that everyone who takes drugs is really bad or anything. I told her I smoke a bit of dope sometimes and she didn't have a go at me or anything – she just listened.'

Augustus, aged 15

New style

More recently drugs education has become more informative. In schools and youth clubs, young people are given the facts about drugs. The idea is that, if we know the effects and attractions as well as the real dangers of drug use, we will be able to make sensible decisions about whether or not to take them.

There are other ways of teaching about drugs, too. In some schools older pupils talk to younger ones about drugs. This can be particularly helpful because young people are more likely to accept advice from people of a similar age. Sometimes drug addicts are invited to talk to children about the reality of being on drugs.

Shock tactics such as comparing a drug user's brain with a fried egg may initially put people off drugs, but many experts don't think it works in the long term.

It's your opinion

Recent research suggests that the media's concentration on a few deaths from taking ecstasy has encouraged many young people to switch to cocaine, a much more harmful drug. Should the media have focused on how these deaths could have been prevented, by 'chilling out' and drinking enough water?

Advertising campaigns

Several governments have tried to use scare tactics in advertising campaigns to dissuade teenagers from even trying drugs. The US Partnership for a Drug-Free America ran a television advert in 1987 depicting fried eggs. The slogan was: 'This is your brain. This is your brain on drugs.' Looking back, many Americans today vividly remember that the advert scared them away from drugs. However, many others felt cheated when they realised that not all drugs were that dangerous, or even felt challenged to take the 'dare' and experiment with drugs.

In 2003, the UK government launched a new drugs education campaign called 'Talk to Frank' with adverts on television and radio. It takes a new, lighter note and is built around a confidential website and chatline that gives well-informed advice, information and support. The idea is to keep teenagers talking to parents or other support groups rather than going off on their own.

Confusing

Sometimes the messages about drugs can be very confusing. It is possible that your parents or carer have taken drugs. If they admit that they have, but then tell you not to do the same, you may feel that they are being unfair.

There are plenty of places to get balanced advice about drugs. If you feel you need to talk to someone about drugs, there are some phone numbers and web addresses at the end of this book.

There is plenty of informed advice about drugs available from experienced counsellors and ex-users. It's just a phone call away.

Giving up drugs

Many people who take illegal drugs decide to stop taking them at some point in their life. This may be because they are concerned about their health or perhaps they are worried about the amount they are spending on drugs. Whatever the reason, there are many people and organisations that can help.

Courtney Love is one of many people who has struggled to kick a hard-drug habit.

Life changes

Sometimes people simply grow out of taking drugs. Most people give up using ecstasy during their twenties. They may have tried drugs when they were younger, but as their lives have moved on they have found enjoyment in other ways. As you get older you are also likely to take on more responsibilities in your life, including a career and starting a family. Drugs can feel like an unwelcome distraction.

It's your decision

Do you want to quit?
If you are a drug user, giving up has to be a decision that you take for yourself – no-one can make you do it. If you decide to give up drugs it may be helpful to contact one of the organisations on page 43 for some advice.

Withdrawal symptoms

If people are addicted to drugs it can be difficult to stop taking them. Drug users who just stop taking drugs altogether often suffer from withdrawal symptoms. These symptoms vary according to the type of drug and how quickly the user 'withdraws'. Withdrawing from heroin has been likened to a nasty bout of 'flu with symptoms like body aches, runny nose and sweating. Quick withdrawal from certain drugs such as barbiturates and tranquillisers can be dangerous, causing rises in blood pressure and temperature, stomach cramps and vomiting.

Going back

Withdrawing from drugs is just the start of the battle against dependence. The ex-user may not be able to tell the difference between anxiety, anger, depression or withdrawal distress. What they do know is that their favourite drug will quickly make them feel 'normal'. Help is needed to resist the temptation to fall back into drug-taking.

Support

Addicts who wish to stop taking drugs are supported in many ways. They can talk to trained counsellors about the reasons for their drug use, and attend self-help groups where they can talk to other drug users.

Rehabilitation centres also play an important role in treatment. They offer addicts a supportive place to live, for between three months and a year, while they are coming off drugs. Several studies show that drug addiction treatment reduces drug use by 40 to 60 per cent. But statistics also show that less than 25 per cent of those who are treated need no further help to stay off drugs.

This woman has just picked up a prescription for methadone, a heroin substitute.

It's your opinion

Do you think addicts deserve sympathy when they are trying to stop taking drugs? Does it serve them right for starting on drugs, or is drug addiction an illness like any other?

Art therapy is one of the many methods used by drug rehabilitation centres.

Methadone

Methadone is a manufactured drug that has similar effects to those of heroin. Doctors sometimes give it to addicts as it is weaker and less addictive than heroin itself, so it can be a useful step towards giving up heroin. Methadone is still dangerous, however, and if users take too much it can kill.

Whichever way an addict chooses to give up drugs, it is never easy and always depends on willpower and hard work.

Drugs and the law

Recreational drugs are illegal, or against the law, in most countries around the world. Punishments for drug use or possession vary from one country to another. In some countries certain drugs are tolerated that are not allowed in others. For example, in Saudi Arabia it is illegal to consume alcohol.

A large proportion of police resources are used to tackle drug crime.

It's your opinion

Two theories suggest that cannabis should not be legalised. The 'gateway' theory says that smoking cannabis places a person in a position where they might be more likely to come across other drugs. The 'stepping stone' theory believes that it is inevitable that people will progress from soft drugs like cannabis to hard drugs like heroin. What do you think?

Why are drugs illegal?

Drugs have not always been illegal, but over the past 100 years or so laws have been passed outlawing them. This is because governments have recognised that drugs can be addictive and believe that they are bad for your health. Religious beliefs often forbid drug use.

In some countries cannabis seeds are legally sold, while in others growing cannabis is illegal.

Punishments

In many countries, punishments for drug use depend on how dangerous they are thought to be. Drugs that are the most dangerous, such as cocaine, crack, ecstasy and heroin, carry the heaviest punishments. If you are caught with these, for example, you might expect a heavy fine or even a prison sentence. Possession of cannabis, on the other hand, might only result in a warning from the police. Sentences for selling drugs are always more severe.

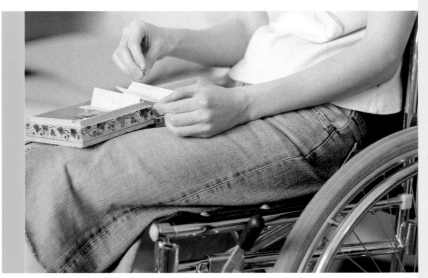

Some people say that cannabis should be legal because it can be a useful form of pain relief for people with illnesses such as arthritis and multiple sclerosis.

Changes in the law

In Portugal the government has decided that personal drug use is no longer a crime. They believe that problem drug use, like addiction, is an illness rather than an offence.

Some people in other countries agree. They say that if drugs were legal they would be less dangerous because scientists would be able to test the purity of drugs in the same way as medicines are tested. Drug users would also be at less risk of being dragged into another world inhabited by illegal drug pushers.

Other people argue that if drugs were legal more people would use them and the rates of drug addiction would rise. This debate is going on all across the world.

The cost of drug use

Illegal drugs can be very expensive. If someone uses a lot it can have a marked impact on how much they have to spend on other things. But drug use has many other, sometimes hidden, costs.

The cost of drugs

If someone spends a lot of their money on a drug habit, they may not have enough to spend on some of the things that make life more enjoyable, like going out, or taking a holiday. If they have a partner or children, they too are likely to suffer because money is short in the family. It was reported in 2003 that up to 350,000 children in the UK are suffering the effects of their parents' drug use.

If someone is addicted to a drug like heroin or crack, the money it takes to feed the habit can run into thousands of pounds each year. People who earn a great deal of money can afford their drug-taking, but many addicts turn to crimes like burglary and muggings to get enough to buy their daily drugs. These crimes have victims who may be extremely upset as a result.

It's your experience

'My nan's flat was burgled by a heroin addict a couple of years ago. They caught him and he was sent to prison for a year but my nan is still serving her sentence – she's scared to go out and hates being in the flat on her own.'

Aldo, aged 14

Many people resort to crime as a way of fuelling a drug habit.

Methamphetamine
weight 3,818 kg.
Value 4,500 million Bht.

The police in Thailand seize massive amounts of illegal drugs each year, but much more leaves the country.

It's your opinion

Over the past few years there has been a steady increase in the number of people caught driving under the influence of drugs. This is partly because the police have only recently recognised this as a problem, but it is also due to the general increase in drug use. Do you think this problem is as serious as drink-driving?

Police resources

Every year police forces around the world have to spend huge amounts of time and resources dealing with illegal drugs and the crimes associated with them. The US customs force calculates that they are only able to check about three per cent of the shipping containers that come into their country each year.

Healthcare

The healthcare system also pays the price of drug use. Millions are spent helping addicts and other drug users, caring for people who have accidents while on drugs and treating those who suffer the ill-effects of drug use. Some people feel that money could have been better spent elsewhere, on treating people who have not risked their health as drug users do.

The after-effects of drug-taking can make it hard to get up in the morning. Many users miss work as a result.

Missing work

Sometimes, if someone takes drugs they may be too tired or unwell to work the next day. In the UK, the effects of drugs and alcohol costs companies almost £3 billion each year. In parts of the world where drug use is particularly high, this can seriously damage the economy of the country.

Drugs in society

Drugs are, or have been, a part of many people's lives for thousands of years. For young people, part of growing up is to try new things and for some this includes experimenting with drugs. Some people carry on taking drugs as they get older and see it as quite a normal part of their lives.

Drugs are much more common in some places like nightclubs.

Drugs and youth culture

In some places, like nightclubs, it is very easy to get hold of drugs and quite a lot of the people there will use them, though of course many will not. Sometimes, if you want to avoid drugs, it is easiest to avoid certain situations. This might include particular parties or mixing with certain people you know use drugs. Remember, there are always plenty of other places you can go where people are enjoying themselves without using drugs.

Drugs in sport

Sport is something that should be all about health and fitness. Teenagers who are involved in sport are much less likely to start using drugs. However, at a professional level, most sports are subject to drug abuse.

Some sports people use drugs such as steroids to help them perform better. Many of these drugs are not illegal but

Drug-taking continually blights professional sports. Here a cyclist is about to undergo a routine drug test.

are banned by sporting authorities because they give the sports person an unfair advantage. Some drugs will build up muscles without exercise, others increase stamina – the ability of the body to keep going. Some of them are also very dangerous if taken over a long period of time. Steroids, for example, can cause heart damage and increase the risk of cancer.

Testing for banned drugs can be very difficult, however. Sometimes when a sports person tests positive for a drug, they claim that they have not taken it or that they took it by mistake.

It's your opinion

Sports people who knowingly take drugs are risking their careers as well as their health. Why do you think they take these risks?

Medicinal drugs

Medicinal drugs are legal drugs that are used to cure and prevent diseases and manage illnesses. There are countless different medicines across the world that are used for a huge variety of reasons.

◀ Medicinal drugs are often produced as tablets or pills.

Medicines

You have probably taken medicines yourself. Some come as tablets and capsules, others are in powder or liquid. They may be swallowed, injected, inhaled or even put on the skin as a cream. As with illegal drugs, to have any effect they have either to enter the bloodstream or be applied directly to a part of the body.

Medicines are made from all sorts of ingredients, including chemicals, plants and animal extracts. In the past, some of the drugs that are illegal today, such as heroin and cocaine, were used for pain relief. Morphine (derived from opium) is still used as a painkiller.

Testing

When a new medicine is invented or discovered it has to be rigorously tested until it is proved safe enough for people to use. Usually drugs are tested on animals first, and then on a group of volunteers. This can take many years. Because of this, new medicines are often very expensive.

It's your opinion

▶ Do you think that taking medicinal drugs to keep you healthy and feeling good is very different from taking illegal drugs for enjoyment? People have been using both for thousands of years. Why do you think that illegal drugs are not considered acceptable, but medicinal ones are?

Some medicines are only available on prescription after you have visited a doctor. Other medicines are considered safe enough to be sold without a prescription.

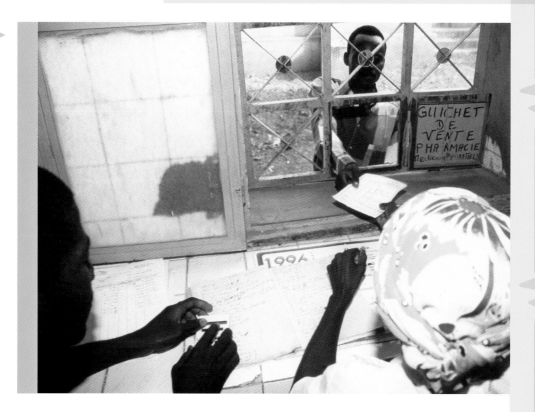

What are they used for?

Medicines are used for numerous other reasons. Maybe you have taken a pill such as paracetamol for a headache, or you've had injections to stop you getting diseases like measles. Medicines are also used for the treatment of cancer, to anaesthetise patients during surgery, to cure infections and to help mental illnesses, such as depression.

Over the years medicinal drugs have saved and improved the lives of millions of people and, because of them, many diseases are no longer such a threat.

It's your experience

'My little brother had meningitis when he was a little baby. The doctors gave him lots of antibiotics to cure him and eventually he got better. Apparently they didn't have antibiotic medicine a hundred years ago and he would almost certainly have died.'

Amy, aged 12

They may not be very pleasant but vaccination drugs have prevented many diseases and saved thousands of lives.

The cost of medicinal drugs

Medicines have been a huge help to us, but they are potentially as dangerous as illegal drugs.

Side-effects

Many medicines have 'side-effects'. This is because when you take the drug it affects other parts of your body as well as the part it is treating. Common side-effects include headaches and tiredness.

Taking more than one medicine at the same time can also have unexpected results and a doctor should always check what you are taking before giving you another drug.

Masking problems

Taking drugs like Prozac for depression can cause problems. For many, the drug will get them over a difficult period in their lives. For others it has the effect of making them feel that everything is fine in their lives when, in truth, action needs to be taken to make their lives better. Then, when they come off the drug, they find they are right back where they began.

Sometimes medicines are not the answer to people's problems. Counselling may be a better alternative.

Allergies

Some people are allergic to certain medicines, and even a small amount of a usually beneficial drug can injure, or in extreme cases, kill them.

Overdose

Some medicines are very dangerous if we take too much of them. This is known as an overdose. Even common painkillers, like paracetamol, are dangerous in this way and can lead to a lingering death through liver failure. It is important to read the product information and only take the size of dose recommended.

It's your experience

'After my dad died, Mum was having difficulty sleeping. The doctor gave her pills to help her sleep better, but after a while she couldn't manage without them. It took her ages to get off them completely and she says she'd never take anything like that again.'

Pete, aged 15

Alison Lapper was born disabled as a result of the drug thalidomide, and spent her childhood in children's homes. She is now a successful international artist.

It's your opinion

Is it fair that life-saving drugs can be so expensive or is it understandable considering how much it costs pharmaceutical companies to make them?

Poor testing

In the 1950s and '60s, pregnant mothers were given a drug called thalidomide to combat 'morning sickness'. This drug had not been tested properly and resulted in many of the mothers giving birth to seriously disabled children.

Addiction

Sometimes medicinal drugs are very addictive. Patients should not be given certain sleeping pills or tranquillisers for more than a few days at a time because it is easy to get hooked on them. Dependence on legal drugs is just as difficult to break as dependence on illegal drugs. In the UK today, more than a million adults are hooked on prescribed anti-depressant drugs.

In 2003, the manufacturers of Seroxat, a widely prescribed anti-depressant, changed the labelling on the medicine. They removed the phrase, 'Remember that you cannot become addicted to Seroxat' after pressure from patients and doctors, who claimed that the drug was indeed addictive.

Hopefully, in the future everyone who needs drugs to treat HIV and AIDS will be able to afford them.

Expensive drugs

Medicinal drugs take many years and millions of pounds to develop. Sometimes the people that need these medicines cannot afford the high prices, and they have to go without.

South Africa has a huge problem with the disease HIV, the virus that can lead to AIDS. An estimated 5.3 million people, more than 12 per cent of South Africa's population, are infected with HIV. The drugs needed to treat it were far too expensive for most sufferers. However, in 2003, protestors won the right to buy the anti-HIV drugs at lower prices.

Alternative treatments

Alternative medicines are drugs and treatments that do not follow the normal scientific rules about drugs. They are sometimes known as complementary medicine.

Acupuncture has been used in the Far East for thousands of years to treat a wide range of illnesses and conditions.

What are they and who uses them?

There are many different alternative medicines. Herbal medicines use plant extracts to treat the same sorts of illnesses as modern medicines. Homeopathy uses highly-diluted plant extracts to treat a wide range of diseases and other conditions. Some therapies don't even use pills or tablets; acupuncture, for example, uses needles placed into particular parts of a patient's body to ease pain and cure symptoms.

No one is really sure how these treatments work, but they have been used for thousands of years and are used by more than one billion people worldwide. One reason for this is that most of the ingredients are cheap and easy to get hold of.

There are thousands of alternative drug treatments available to buy without a prescription.

It's your experience

'I was feeling quite down and depressed and I went to see my doctor about it. She said I could go on anti-depressants but she would prefer me to try St John's Wort first. It's made from a plant, which grows in the garden and is thought to be very safe. I tried it and soon felt better, but I don't know if that was the medicine or not.'

Tina, aged 19

Are they safe? Do they work?

Alternative treatments have been gaining in popularity in Western countries over recent years. Some people like the fact that many of these medicines treat the whole person rather than just particular parts of the body. Others feel that these treatments are much safer than modern medicines.

Many doctors and scientists are still against alternative medicines. They argue that the treatments often only work because the patients believe they will work and that the effects are 'all in the mind'. They also point out that many of the medicines come from the same ingredients as modern medicines and therefore have to be used just as carefully. Digoxin, which is made from the foxglove, has been used since the mid-18th century and is currently given to patients with heart problems.

It's your decision

Would you try alternative medicines? Some people prefer to avoid using any medicines but look to prevention through overall fitness and diet.

Herbs, flowers, fungi and animal extracts are among the ingredients used in some alternative medicines.

New drugs

Across the world laws and attitudes towards drugs are changing. Both illegal drugs and medicinal drugs are also changing and new ones are being created all the time.

Dealers are always adding new drugs to their supply lists. Here, Alex Krassenberg poses in his business called 'Dr. Paddo, The Natural Drug Store,' in the Netherlands. Krassenberg's business offers home delivery of magic mushrooms, herbal ecstasy, organic 'designer drugs' and at least 600 other drugs.

New illegal drugs

In the 1980s previously unheard of drugs like ecstasy became popular with some young people. This was partly because of the start of a new club scene, where the drugs were used. No one can predict what changes in youth culture there may be in years to come, or what effect thse changes may have on drug use.

Future drug-taking

Many people feel that the penalties for using certain drugs, like cannabis, are too harsh. This has led to a change in the law in some countries. Maybe, one day, some of the drugs that are illegal now will not be against the law. It may be that taking drugs will be seen as a perfectly normal and socially acceptable behaviour. In 1997 Noel Gallagher, singer with the British band Oasis, famously claimed that taking drugs was no more out of the ordinary than drinking a cup of tea. He had to retract his comments following outrage in the press, but do you think his comments might hold any truth in the future?

MRSA is an infection that is resistant to common antibiotics. New medicines need to be developed to treat it and other new diseases as they emerge.

Medicines

New medicinal drugs are constantly being developed to tackle the problems of modern life. Drug companies are trying to develop medicines that can be used to control our weight, or cure illnesses like cancer and the common cold. They are also trying to make safe and effective anti-depressants since depression and other mental illnesses are a growing threat to health. New alternative therapies are also being developed, to add to the wide range already available.

A word of warning

Unfortunately, some of the medicines we already have are starting to lose their powers to cure. Antibiotics, which treat bacterial infections and have saved so many lives over the past 50 years, have been overused, sometimes for the wrong illnesses. This has caused certain bacteria to change so that antibiotics no longer kill them. If doctors and patients are not more careful in the future, we may not continue to benefit from the healing powers of this medicine.

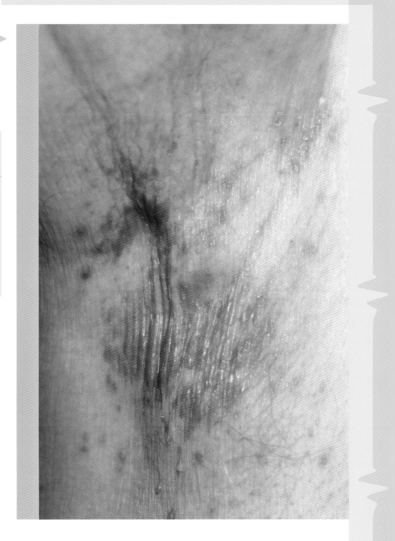

Some drugs, however, are experiencing a new lease of life. Aspirin, originally only used as a medicine for pain relief, has now been found to help prevent heart attacks. Research is also being carried out into whether aspirin can prevent some types of cancer.

Drugs and your life

At some point in your life you will find yourself in a situation where illegal drugs are available. It may have already happened. It's up to you to decide whether drug use will be part of your life. As with anything, it's always best to make the most informed decision you can.

Sports and other hobbies are activities we can really take pleasure in with our friends. ▼

Pressure

When you are growing up there can be pressure from friends and even members of your family to try new things. If you do take drugs, remember it is your mind and body that they are going to affect and it is your responsibility to say 'No' if you don't want them.

If you feel concerned about responding to pressure from other people, there are some things you can do:

1. Rehearse on your own what you will say.
2. Avoid the places where you are likely to be offered drugs.
3. Spend less time with friends who take drugs and more with friends who don't.

Even more than healthcare, these children need a decent family home and enough food to eat. ▶

It's your opinion

Poverty is the most deadly disease in the world; and millions of children die each year in the poorer countries of the world because they don't have clean drinking water, proper housing and enough food to eat. Do you think it would be a good idea if some of the money spent on new medicines were used instead to tackle poverty?

Alternatives

Medicines always carry some risks and they are not the only way to prevent illness. Avoiding smoking and other dangerous activities are obvious ways of keeping healthy, as is eating a healthy diet.

Exercising regularly not only makes your body healthy but can also make you feel good. This is because your body releases chemicals called endorphins when you exercise, and these make you feel relaxed and happy. The same chemicals are released when you dance.

It's your experience

'I used to take cocaine at the weekends and smoked cannabis every day. I stopped when one of my mates started doing heroin; I was really worried I was going to go the same way. What I didn't realise was that life would be so much better without drugs. I've got more energy and I'm actually getting somewhere with my life now. I've got a job and a girlfriend and things are going really well.'

Zack, aged 18

◀ For most people, a balanced life of work and leisure is the most rewarding. Illegal drugs don't really add anything positive to anyone's life.

41

Glossary

Addict someone who feels a physical or mental need to do something, such as take drugs

Amphetamine a stimulant drug that comes in powder or tablet form. Also called speed

Antibiotic a medicine used to treat bacterial infections

Carcinogenic something that causes cancer

Depression a medical condition when someone feels sad and uninterested in life.

Hallucinogenic something which can cause people to think they see something that is not really there

Hepatitis an infectious disease that affects the liver

HIV an infection that lead to AIDS, a potentially fatal disease that affects the body's immune system

Inhaled breathed in

Inject to use a needle and syringe to push a drug into the bloodstream

Measles an infectious disease that can lead to serious complications including breathing problems and brain damage

Meningitis a disease that causes a potentially fatal inflammation of the coating of the brain

Overdose when too much of a drug, either legal or illegal, is taken, perhaps because it is too pure. It can lead to severe illness or even death

Paranoia to suspect and distrust people for no good reason

Prescribed when a doctor gives a patient medicine

Psychological to do with how someone thinks and feels

Stimulant a substance that speeds up the way the brain works

Steroids chemicals that can help build muscle

Stoned a slang term for how it feels when someone takes drugs

Symptoms the signs that something has happened, such as a reaction to taking drugs

Tranquilliser a medicine that calms a person down

Vapours the gases given off from a substance

Further information

UK

DrugScope
A leading centre of expertise on drugs.

32-36 Loman Street, London SE1 0EE
Tel: 020 7928 1211
Website: www.drugscope.org.uk

Talk to Frank
Informal and confidential advice about drugs. Calls are free and lines are open 24 hours a day.

Tel: 0800 776600
Website: www.talktofrank.com

Drugs-info
Help for people who have family members who use drugs, including information about drugs and their effects.

Website: www.drugs-info.co.uk

Parents Against Drug Abuse
Information for parents concerned about drugs.

12-14 Church Parade
Ellesmere Port, Cheshire CH65 2ER
Tel: 08457 023867
Website: www.btinternet.com/~padahelp

The Site
Information about drugs and other issues concerning young people.

www.thesite.org.uk

ADFAM
Offers information to families of drug and alcohol users, and the website has a database of local family support services.

Waterbridge House, 32-36 Loman Street
London SE1 0EE
Tel: 020 7928 8898
Email: admin@adfam.org.uk
Website: www.adfam.org.uk

Re-Solv (Society for the Prevention of Solvent and Volatile Substance Abuse)
A national charity providing information for parents and young people.

30A High Street,
Staffordshire ST15 8AW
Tel: 01785 817885
Helpline: 0808 8002345
Email: information@re-solv.org
Website: www.re-solv.org

AUSTRALIA

Australian Drug Information Network
Contains drug information and links to other Australian drug-related sites.

PO Box 818
North Melbourne, VIC 3051
Tel: (03) 9278 8100
Website: www.adin.com.au

Note to parents and teachers: Because of the nature of the subject matter and the Internet, these websites may contain material that is inappropriate for some young people. We therefore strongly advise that Internet access is supervised by a responsible adult.

Index